THE AWESOME PHYSICS
IN YOUR CITY

WRITTEN BY **THE AMAZING THEATRE OF PHYSICS**
ILLUSTRATED BY **TOMÁŠ KOPECKÝ**

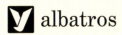

DISCOVER PHYSICS...

1. In the Street 4
2. On a Construction Site 8
3. At the Amusement Park 12
4. In a Restaurant 16
5. At the Playground 20
6. At a Concert 24
7. At the Pool 28
8. At the Sports Field 32
9. At the Doctor's 36
10. In a Shop 40
Glossary 44

1. IN THE STREET

An ambulance wailing, a car honking its horn, a drill buzzing... Everywhere you look, the street is full of noise, movement, and sensations. It's a lot to take in, but if you look around, you might be surprised by all the interesting things you can find in the street.

ELECTRICITY

Lightning on cables

Hey, have you ever seen any trams in your city? If so, you might have noticed something cool on dark nights: a quick flash of light and a soft rumble near the wires above. This happens when the poles on the tram drift a bit away from the cables. It's like what happens during a storm. There's so much electricity in those cables that it can jump through the air onto the nearby poles, making a neat show!

ELECTRICITY

Underground

Beneath the surface of the pavement or a road lies a hidden world waiting to be unearthed. A city is a labyrinth of sewers, pipes, and cables intricately woven together, allowing us to turn on water taps, illuminate our homes, and cook dinner on a cozy gas stove. But imagine if all these essential lifelines were exposed. It wouldn't be very practical, would it? That's why everything is cleverly hidden underground, keeping our cityscapes uncluttered and safe for all.

Seeing around corners

Sometimes when we're driving through crossroads or bends in the road, our view is blocked by buildings or tall fences, making it tricky to see very far ahead. That's where rounded mirrors come in! Have you ever noticed how they stick out? They're shaped like inverted spoons, so we can see much more than with flat mirrors. Light bounces off the mirror from around the corner and reflects towards us.

LIGHT

Blaring sirens

Ever noticed how when a vehicle comes towards you, its sound changes? You might hear it most clearly when an ambulance rushes by, siren blaring. As it zooms closer, the pitch gets higher. But as it moves away, the pitch drops lower. This is just how sound works when things move closer or farther apart. It's called the Doppler effect. And guess what? It's not just sound that does this; light does too. Astronomers detect this exact kind of shift in light. It helps them know if stars are moving closer or farther away – which, believe it or not, is how we know how old the universe is. Amazing, right?

A rainbow on the road

Sometimes, after it's been raining, you might spot a rainbow on the road. Unfortunately, this kind of rainbow forms on spilled oil spreading over a puddle. Light interacts with it, creating different colors based on the oil's thickness. It's like the rainbow streaks you see when blowing bubbles.

The loud experiment

Ready for a noisy experiment? You can change the pitch of a sound right in your own home! Just grab your phone and download a "tone generator" app. Then, grab a pair of your mother's tights and place your phone at one end. Now, spin it above your head and listen closely. As the tights spin, the pitch of the sound will go up and down, just like a siren!

It sounds much better this way.

Staying safe on the road

The most important thing about road safety is for cars, cyclists, and pedestrians to notice each other. To stay safe, it's helpful to know the answers to these two questions: How can I be seen even when it's dark? And how long does it take for a car to stop?

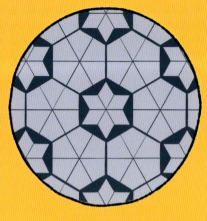

A reflector close up.

How a reflector reflects light, as viewed from the side.

Corner mirrors

The best way to be seen on the road, whether it's day or night, is by wearing what are called retroreflectors. These include reflectors on bikes, reflective bands, and strips on bags and jackets. On construction sites, it's a must for folks to wear high-visibility vests and helmets. But what makes them so easy to see? Just look at a shiny reflector.

Take a really close look at one sometime. Inside it, you'll see lots of tiny structures that reflect light really well. They're actually like tiny mirrors! Because there are three of them arranged in a clever way, they always bounce light back to exactly where it came from. So, if you shine a flashlight on a reflector, the light will come right back to you.

TO SEE AND BE SEEN

If someone dressed in black appears in front of a car at night, they can be really hard to see. But if they're wearing a reflector or a reflective strip, it reflects the light from the headlights right back to the driver. The driver can then avoid them in time.

Nobody could miss seeing me!

Before a car stops

When it comes to cars, we must be super careful. Even though you can easily see a car when you're walking, you can never be sure that the driver sees you. And when the driver starts to brake, it still takes a while for the car to come to a complete stop. Even a car traveling slowly through town can take as much as 100 feet to stop.

BRAKING

If a driver slams on the brakes, the wheels can start to skid on the road and the driver could lose control of the car. This can be really bad when it rains. That's why car tires have grooves that let water escape from under the tire. The deeper the grooves, the more water can escape. But these grooves wear down with use, and if the tires get too smooth, they need to be replaced with new ones.

SLIPPERY WHEN WET

When it's rainy or there's snow and ice, tires don't grip the road as well, and it takes longer to stop. That's why, if it's raining, you should be much more careful crossing the road and preferably wait until all the cars have gone by. It's even worse on ice, which is why in countries where it snows and temperatures drop below freezing, cars are fitted with special winter tires. These have an even deeper pattern of grooves to grip the snow better and brake more quickly.

SPEED

What has the biggest effect on how a car brakes is how fast it's going. The faster a car is moving, the longer it takes to stop. Speed becomes more important the faster you're traveling. Just look at the numbers. When a car is traveling at 30 miles an hour on a dry road in town, it will stop after about 115 feet. Outside of town, if a car is traveling at 60 miles an hour, it will stop after about 320 feet. The speed has doubled but the braking distance is much more than twice as long. With higher speed you need much more braking distance than one would expect. That's why the speed limit in towns is often reduced to 30 miles an hour – so that drivers can stop faster if they need to.

I've lost control... Every man for himself!

So always remember to be extra careful around cars. Always make sure the driver can see you, and always wait until all the cars have stopped before crossing the road – whether it's in the rain, in the snow, on highways, or on any old ordinary day.

2. ON A CONSTRUCTION SITE

The bustle of construction work never stops in cities – something's always being built. It's a marvelous sight, especially when it involves big yellow diggers, bulldozers, and other machines.

Racket, din, and noise

As soon as you step onto a construction site, the noise hits you hard. All those machines, diggers, bulldozers, and pneumatic drills make a real racket. Listening to loud noises for too long can hurt our ears. That's why it's so important for construction workers to wear earmuffs.

SOUND

No helmet, no entry

PRESSURE

Every worker on a construction site has to wear a helmet to protect their head. But how does it do that? Inside the hollow plastic shell, you'll find a couple of plastic straps. When you bump your head, these straps spread the impact to a larger area so it gives your head just a gentle squeeze. For the helmet to work, it must fit closely around your head. That's why you shouldn't wear a helmet that doesn't fit you properly and you should always fasten it tightly.

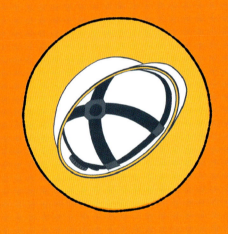

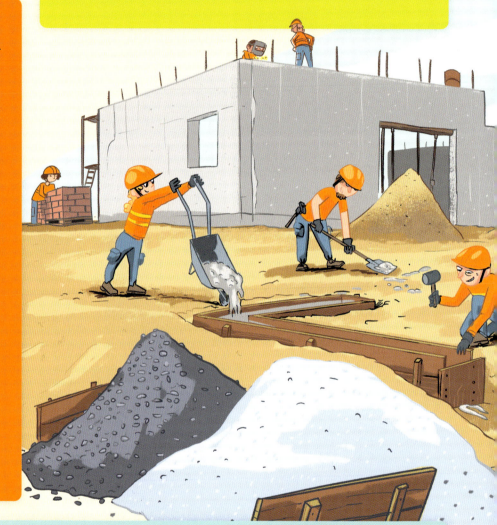

Piles of sand

EQUILIBRIUM

On a construction site, there are usually piles of different materials. You'll find sand, gravel, and sometimes even rocks. But each pile has a different angle of steepness. When you pour sand out of a bag, it always forms the same cone shape. Each type of material forms a pile with a different steepness. Sand and gravel, as well as sugar, salt, and flour, always form their own unique cone shape when you pour them out.

dry sand 34°   crushed gravel 45°

lentils 25°– 35°   flour 35°– 45°

FORCES

"Copycat!"

"Looks like hard work."

An excavator's arm

Digging a hole takes a lot of work. But instead of slaving away doing it by hand, it's much better to leave it to a machine called a digger. If you watch a digger digging, you might notice how similar its arm is to a human arm. A digger also has a shoulder, an elbow, and a wrist. The difference is the digger has a bucket at the end instead of a hand. Each of the excavator's joints has a piston that can extend or contract to bend or straighten the joint. An excavator gets by with just one piston for each joint, while our arms need two different muscles for each joint. One muscle bends the arm, the other straightens it. We can only shorten our muscles; we can't lengthen them.

How much can a wall bear?

The bricks we use to build houses are often riddled with holes. Inside them are hollow tubes filled with air, which help to trap heat inside the house. Most importantly, a brick must be sturdy, as the bottom row of masonry bears the weight of everything above it. So, even a brick with cavities in it can support a hefty load from top to bottom. But if you were to lay it on its side, the brick wouldn't support your weight without breaking. However, that doesn't matter, as the bricks in a wall only experience pressure from the top down, never from the sides. So, as long as you put them in the wall the right way, it's totally safe!

PRESSURE

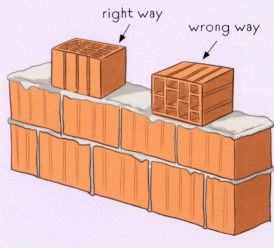

right way — wrong way

WORK

Slow but strong

Every type of work follows the same rule – either we have to put in a lot of effort or we can be fast. If you're carrying a light backpack, you can run easily. But if you have to lug around a ton of heavy shopping bags, you'll have to take it slow. Machines are similar to people in this way. If they need to handle heavy work, they have to do it super slowly. That's why diggers, bulldozers, cranes, and steamrollers move at a snail's pace.

Save yourself some work

The biggest challenge on every construction site is pretty much the same. As the building grows taller, we obviously need to lift heavy building materials higher and higher. It was like that back when they were building the Great Pyramids in Egypt, and guess what? It's still the same today! Even though technology keeps getting better, the tricks we use haven't changed much.

Push and pull

If you have to hoist something up high using a rope, a pulley will be super handy. The pulley itself doesn't do the work for you – it just changes where you need to pull. Imagine you're up high and need to pull up a heavy bucket from below. If you try to pull it up directly with just the rope, it's going to be tough. But if you hang the rope over a pulley, you can stand back and pull the rope down. It's way easier this way because you can use your full weight to pull down on the rope. Pulleys can even give you more power – you just need more of them. If you hang the bucket from another pulley that's not attached to anything, you'll only need half the force suddenly. But your rope has to be twice as long. Once again, you're trading force for distance. You pull with less force, but on a longer rope.

An uphill task

It's super simple. Lifting a big chunk of rock three feet high is hard work. But pushing it three feet up a gentle slope is much easier. You have a choice: apply a lot of force for a short time or just a little force but for longer. There's always a trade-off. If you make the job easier in one way, it'll become more difficult in another way.

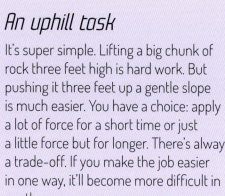

A wheel with a handle

Once you've tried a pulley, is there another way to boost your power? You bet! You can start winding up the rope using something called a winch. It's super strong and perfect for lifting heavy stuff. A winch has an axle – a pole to wind the rope onto – and a crank to turn the axle. The axle needs to be thin, and the crank needs to be really wide. That way, you get the most power. It's still the same idea at play. The thin axle gets spun in a small circle with a lot of force. The big crank turns in a large circle, but you use less force.

The crank can only be turned one way.

A COGWHEEL

To make a winch even better, you can add a cogwheel. It's like a gear with teeth, kind of like a saw. The teeth slope up at an angle and then straight back down. On the opposite side of these teeth is a lever with a little hook that fits between the teeth. This setup lets the cogwheel turn in only one direction, because the teeth lock in place in the other direction. It's a cool trick because if you stop cranking, the thing you're lifting won't fall since the cogwheel won't spin the other way.

A RATCHET

A cogwheel that only moves one way is super helpful. In a workshop, there's a special wrench called a ratchet. It tightens nuts or bolts when you turn it in one direction, but it spins freely the other way. This means you don't have to keep taking it off and putting it back on like you do with a regular wrench. You'll see the same kind of ratchet on straps used to tie stuff together on a construction site. It keeps the strap from getting loose after you've tightened it. Even your bike uses this idea! When you pedal, the chain turns little wheels called sprockets on the back wheel. When you stop pedaling, these wheels let go, and you hear a click from the back wheel, giving you a break.

3. AT THE AMUSEMENT PARK

In some European countries, amusement parks are called "luna parks." This name comes from American, though – from Luna Park, which opened on Coney Island in New York in 1903. Even though real trips to the moon wouldn't happen until many years later, people still loved visiting these parks. So why are these parks so awesome, and how do they work?

SPEED

The roller coaster

Did you know cars on the highway can go up to 80 miles per hour, while planes can reach 500 miles per hour? And get this: the Earth itself is zooming around the Sun at a whopping 67,000 miles per hour! By comparison, roller coasters aren't very fast. So, speed alone isn't what makes them so thrilling – it's the sudden changes in speed and direction. On a roller coaster, you'll go from fast to slow, and twist and turn in all sorts of wild ways, all in just a few minutes. That's what gets your heart pumping.

ENERGY TRANSFORMATIONS

The pirate ship

On this exhilarating ride, you'll feel weightless one moment and then relieved the next as you swing back and forth, up and down. A motor rocks the ship, but it's good old-fashioned gravity that makes the ride truly exciting. It speeds up on its way down, using the gathered velocity to swing you back up again. At the highest point, you might feel like you're about to float away, but fear not! The ship rises and falls with you. If you lift out of your seat a little, the ship will always catch you. So hold on tight and enjoy the ride!

"Woo, I feel light as a feather."

"Hey, how's the view up there?!"

FORCES

Bumper cars

Bumper cars offer two exciting challenges. First, you can test your skill by avoiding crashes. With a bit of clever maneuvering, you can outrun everyone else on the track. Each car gets its power from an electric grid above the track, so they all have the same speed. The second thrill is bumping into as many cars as you can! The most intense bumps happen when two cars collide head-on at full speed. The smallest bumps occur when you gently tap the car in front of you, moving at a similar pace.

A full-on collision.

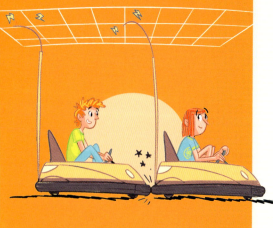

A slight bump.

LIGHT

In the neon glow

An amusement park is full of colorful neon lights. Surprisingly, these neon tubes, like the ones at the park, were developed shortly after the first amusement park opened its gates. They operate much like the fluorescent lights found in classrooms. Inside these tubes, there's only a trace of neon gas. Tiny particles called electrons whiz around inside, colliding with the neon atoms and transferring energy to them. This energy causes the neon to emit a red glow. If a different gas fills the tube, it produces a different colored glow.

13

To get things moving

At an amusement park there's pandemonium everywhere you look. Everything's shaking, spinning, and swinging. But what sets all of this stuff in motion?

MUSCLES

Many fairground rides are powered by the visitors themselves, so we can't forget this type of "propulsion" (which is just a fancy word for moving something forward). You'll notice this on the swinging ships, the umbrella ride, or the pedal cars. Basically, human muscle power is an even bigger money-spinner than gravity. People pay for their tickets and yet they provide their own energy.

ELECTRICITY

You'll often see an electric motor at an amusement park – like in the bumper cars. At home, you'll find them in drills, blenders, and fans – anywhere electricity makes something spin.

FUEL

Traveling carnivals go from town to town using the power of car engines. Inside these engines, fuel is constantly exploding. In a garden shed, you'll find similar combustion engines in chainsaws and lawnmowers.

No such thing as a free ride

At amusement parks, one of the most exciting ways to make something move is by letting it drop. To use gravity for this thrill, the ride first needs to be lifted up. Different types of propulsion are used to hoist it. Once it's at the top, gravity takes care of the fun part. That's why most roller coaster cars are pulled up to the highest point first. After that, they zoom down, speed up, slow down, and twist around, all thanks to gravity.

The thrill of inertia

Why do people love riding swing carousels (aka chair swing rides) so much? Well, a big part of the fun comes from inertia – the physical force that keeps things moving in a straight line until another force changes it.

ON AND ON
As the swing carousel spins, you feel pulled outward and pressed against your seat. That's inertia at work. It's not just you – everything around you has it too. It tries to keep things as they are, resisting speeding up, slowing down, or turning. So, you need strength to overcome it. When biking, squeezing the brakes halts the bike, but what stops you? Inertia wants you to keep moving, potentially launching you forward. Your arm strength is what keeps you steady and safe.

STRAIGHT ON AND ROUND THE BEND
The swing carousel spins because chains pull on the seat to keep it moving. If one of these chains were to break, the seat could go flying straight out of the carousel! But don't worry – the restraints are there to keep you safe. They press against you from the side, making sure you stay with the seat as it spins. So when you feel like something's trying to throw you out of the carousel, it's actually just your inertia at work, trying to keep you moving in a straight line.

A STOMACH-CHURNING RIDE
Inertia adds excitement to other rides too. Take a roller coaster: as it reaches the top of the slope and sharply turns downward, inertia is what keeps you moving up a bit longer. Then comes that dizzying yet thrilling drop that makes your stomach lurch!

4. IN A RESTAURANT

In a restaurant, there are always lots of delicious foods and drinks to enjoy. During family meals or coffee breaks, there's always something new to try. Next time you go out to eat, here are some fun physics facts you can share with everyone.

Drinking through a straw

Sipping through a straw is always a delight! It's fun to watch your drink climb higher and higher up the straw. But did you ever wonder how high it can go? Well, here on Earth, there's a limit: about 30 feet. Even if you give it all your might, you can't make it go any higher. Why? It is actually Earth's atmosphere that is pressing the drink up the straw. If there were more of the air above us, you'd be able to drink from a straw even more than 30 feet tall.

PRESSURE

Loads of bubbles

Bubbles in fizzy drinks aren't just for show – they add flavor! But they're not regular air; they're what's called carbon dioxide gas, packed in under high pressure. This gas slips in between water molecules. Surprisingly, there can be as much CO_2 as there is drink! Ever notice bubbles clinging to the sides of your glass? It's easier for them to escape there. Try adding a pinch of salt – the bubbles will rush out because they have more surfaces to cling to.

PRESSURE

Who's up for some coffee?

There's an art to making a good cup of coffee, even if you're too young to realize it yet. But you can still notice how coffee naturally forms layers. When you add milk to your mom's coffee, it sits at the bottom before blending in. With skill, you can turn it into a latte macchiato. Pour warm milk first, then carefully add the coffee, and finish with frothy milk on top. Do you know why the layers in coffee are arranged this way?

The (un)spilt experiment

Let's play magician! Fill a glass to the brim with water. Cut out a piece of card or stiff plastic film to cover the glass. Carefully turn the glass upside-down while holding the card in place. Slowly release your grip on the card – it'll stay put as if by magic! But be cautious; try this over a sink because accidents can happen. There's a very thin layer of water between the edge of the glass and the card that won't let any air in, so the water has no way to get out.

Pour yourself a cuppa

Whenever you pour a hot cup of tea, the hot water swiftly changes color as it's poured over the tea bag. But if you accidentally use cold water, you'll notice it's slower and often only the bottom changes color. In hot water, particles move faster, carrying tea with them, while in cold water, everything moves slower, allowing tea to settle. That's why stirring sugar in cold water takes longer, while it dissolves more easily in warm water.

Cool it down... but how?

When we want to cool something down, we use various methods. You wouldn't want to put ice directly into your soup, right? It's much better to blow on it instead. But why?

It's hot!

You know how it goes: sometimes soup is too hot to handle – it burns your tongue. We see steam rising from it because the fastest particles are escaping as gas, cooling off the soup. When you blow on the surface, though, you whisk away the hot steam, allowing other particles to escape faster. But watch out if there's a lot of grease on the surface – it blocks evaporation, and the soup stays hot. By the way, using a wide dish for your soup helps too. In a deep bowl, the surface area is smaller, so steam escapes more slowly.

Hot soup

A wide dish · A deep bowl

Soft drinks with ice

In summertime, blowing on fizzy drinks won't do much to cool them down. Adding ice is the way to go, although it does mean sacrificing some space in your glass for the drink. But here's the interesting part: keep an eye on the level as the ice melts. Does it go up or down? The answer depends on the drink's density compared to water. In pure water, melting ice doesn't change the level at all.

How cold will it get?

Imagine pouring 80°F water into a glass, then adding the same amount of 60°F water. You might think the final temperature would be 70°F, and you'd be right. However, if you mix 80°F water with the same amount of *ice* (not water) at 32°F, the final temperature of the water will not be in the middle. It will drop almost down to the temperature of the ice – 32°F. That's because melting ice needs a lot of energy, making the water much cooler.

What floats where?

If you want to see how things float, just look at a table that's been set for a meal. In every cup and on every plate, things follow the same rules about density – density simply means how tightly packed something is. Just remember, *dense* doesn't mean heavy.

Density

The density of a thing depends on what it's made of – the weight of its atoms and how closely packed they are. For example, a spoon made of metal sinks quickly in water due to its high density. However, when we consider what floats, it's not just about weight. A tiny pin will sink like a spoon, while huge icebergs, despite their massive size, float. The reason is because ice has a lower density than a pin, despite being so much bigger. Similarly, when you make tea, a tea bag, full of air, takes time to sink, while sugar or honey sinks quickly and needs to be stirred. The same principle applies in soup: heavier ingredients sink, while oil (less dense than water) floats on top, leaving greasy spots.

Please ladle it up from the bottom.

The cocktail experiment

Let's experiment with density! Grab a glass and pour in different liquids according to their density. Start with thick ketchup, then add syrup, water and perhaps some oil on top. Don't forget to garnish your cocktail! Try to find something that floats in each layer. It can be challenging to find something for the oil layer; a plastic lid might work. Now, for the exciting part: drop two items into the cocktail, one small and one big, but otherwise the same, like pieces of carrot or apple. Will the bigger piece sink lower because it's heavier? Or will the smaller piece push its way down through the layers? Let's find out together!

5. AT THE PLAYGROUND

Playgrounds are full of fun activities like swinging, spinning, sliding, and climbing. After a whole day of playing and running around, you're exhausted, right? Well you can give your brain a workout too. Thinking about the best way to approach the playground can make it even more fun and interesting.

Feeling dizzy

Riding on a merry-go-round can feel like a whirlwind! Although there's no invisible monster trying to pull us off, we need to really hold on tight to stay on. The farther away you sit from the middle, the tighter you need to grip. You see, when you're farther out, you turn in a larger circle. You move faster than in the center part. So you have to hold on tighter. So, hold on tight and enjoy the dizzying spins of the merry-go-round!

FORCES

Climbing up into the clouds

Scaling a climbing wall is quite the adventure! It requires not only strong arms and legs but also careful thinking. Grip is key to prevent slipping, so having sturdy shoes with rubber toes for your feet is essential. However, keeping a good hold with your hands can be trickier, especially when they get sweaty. That's where climbers use chalk, a white powder that greatly increases friction, helping your hands grip the wall better.

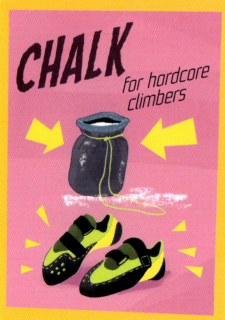

CHALK for hardcore climbers

EQUILIBRIUM

Sticking to the wall

Climbers are careful to keep their body as close to the wall as possible. When you're climbing try to do the same. The farther you are from the wall, the more strain on your arms and the quicker they tire. Remember the three-point method for safety: always keep three of your limbs securely positioned on holds while moving the fourth. Wait until it's secure before freeing up another hand or foot. Holding on in only two places makes it easier to lose balance.

SPEED

How to dress for a slide

Wearing the right clothing (like pants) makes sliding down the chute a breeze. But if you're wearing shorts and sliding mainly on your bare legs, you won't glide as smoothly. Not only will you go slower, but you might even get painful friction burns as your skin sticks to the metal. That's also why water pours down a water slide – to reduce friction and make the ride more fun.

ENERGY TRANSFORMATIONS

Slow going up, quick coming down

Climbing up all the steps to the top of a slide can be quite the workout. But the higher the slide, the better the ride down. Every bit of energy you put into climbing up is returned to you by the slide, even if some of it is lost to friction. The same principle applies to riding a bike. It's tough work pedaling up a big hill, but the thrill of coasting back down makes it worthwhile. However, it's a different story when you exert a lot of energy lifting something heavy, only for it to slip and come crashing down on your foot.

FORCES

21

Seesaws and scissors

Cooperation and coordination are key when two people ride a seesaw, especially if they're different sizes. The heavier person should sit closer to the middle, while the lighter person should sit at the very end. This positioning helps balance the seesaw and requires less effort to bounce back up. You can understand this concept by trying to open a door close to the hinges – it's much harder than using the handle. Similarly, scissors work best when held away from the pivot point in the middle and the thing being cut is held close to the pivot point. To maximize cutting force, different cutting tools, like pliers and garden shears, are designed with short blades and long handles. For delicate tasks, long scissors are better, as they provide precision rather than force.

"How come she's suddenly so strong?"

How do swings work?

Swinging on a swing can feel exhilarating, especially when you lean back and it feels like you might fly away. Have you ever noticed the air hitting you as you swing higher and higher? Well, it's this air that gradually slows you down, eventually bringing the swing to a stop. To keep swinging, you need someone to give you a push. But as you know, even without help, you can get the swing going by yourself – just lean back and then stretch your legs out in front of you over and over again. This propels you farther and higher, using your energy to swing faster – back and forth, up and down. Each swing has its own rhythm. By finding it, you can make your swinging stronger and reach impressive heights. This principle applies elsewhere too, like when carrying a bowl of soup. If it starts sloshing too much, changing your pace can prevent spills.

Architects use similar principles to make sure tall buildings and long bridges don't sway in strong winds or earthquakes. Remember, the longer the swing, the longer it takes to swing back and forth. So, if you're hanging a swing from a tree, choose one of the highest branches for maximum swinging fun!

6. AT A CONCERT

All sound is the result of vibrations, which can range from very faint to so strong they make things move on a table. But where does sound come from? And how do we hear it?

Flute

Wind instruments, such as flutes, clarinets, saxophones, trumpets, and trombones, work by controlling the air you blow into them. The easy ones, like recorders, need air blown through a small hole against a sharp edge. You blow – and music comes out. Flutes are a little harder, though. To play a flute, you have to shape the air with your lips just right. You can even try it yourself – blowing down into a glass bottle is almost like playing a flute.

Head of a flute

Drums

Every musical instrument makes the air around it move in some way. For example, when you hit a drum, the drum skin ripples like a wave. You can make a drum sound different by tightening or loosening the skin.

Violin

A violin has strings, but you don't usually play them with your fingers. Instead, violinists use a bow. If you were to slow down the bow a lot, you'd see how it catches on a string and pulls at it. Then, it breaks free, and the string springs back, only for the bow to catch it again. When this happens over and over, you'll hear the lovely sound that string instruments make.

Saxophone

A saxophone has a sturdy mouthpiece with a thin piece of wood called a reed stuck to it. You hold this between your teeth and blow into the space between the reed and the mouthpiece. The saxophone has many keys for making high and low notes, but you can also change the pitch by adjusting how hard you blow and how you hold the reed. Oboe and bassoon players use two reeds instead of one. They blow between them like you do if you've ever "played" a blade of grass.

Guitar

A guitar has strings that you can pluck with your fingers or play with a pick. When you play, the strings vibrate so quickly they look like a blur. Thicker strings make lower notes, while thinner strings make higher notes. You can also make a higher note by stretching the string more or by pressing it down on the fretboard to make the string shorter, as shorter strings make higher notes.

Trumpet

Trumpeters (like all brass players) face their own challenge. Simply blowing into a trumpet won't produce any sound. A trumpeter has to control their breath using their lips. It's similar to when you try to imitate a horse whinnying, with your lips flopping around as you exhale – but much faster and with firmer lips. A skilled trumpeter can create enough notes for an entire song just by using their lips!

Trumpet mouthpiece

The D string keeps going out of tune.

TA-DAAAH!

Piano

A piano makes sounds similar to a guitar – by using strings. Each key on a piano is connected to a small hammer. When you press a key, the hammer hits a string, making a sound. Every key has its own string. Thin strings are quieter than thick ones, so there are often two or three thin strings for each note. A piano is basically just a cabinet filled with strings. To keep all the strings tight, it needs a cast-iron frame. That's why pianos are so heavy.

Reed of a saxophone

Double reed of an oboe

Singing and listening

Sound

When we say sound is vibration, we mean it's created from things moving rapidly, to and fro. But what is actually vibrating? Every musical instrument has a part that moves the air around it. Air can't ripple up and down like the sea – it can only contract or expand, in and out like an accordion. So, for air, sound means getting thicker and thinner. Sound can also travel through water. Whales sing underwater, and dolphins use reflections in sound – called echolocation – to find their way. Sound travels through solid objects too. If you put your ear on a table and knock, you'll hear sounds clearly. Quite simply, sound can be anywhere something can vibrate. That's why you wouldn't hear anything in the empty void of space.

Speakers

At big concerts with lots of people, it would be tough to hear the instruments and voices without help, which is why we use speakers to make the sound louder. Inside speakers, there are magnets and coils with paper cones attached. When electricity flows through the coil, it creates a magnetic field that makes the coil move, along with the paper cone. This movement pushes the air and creates sound. When speakers need to be really loud, the paper cone has to move a lot too.

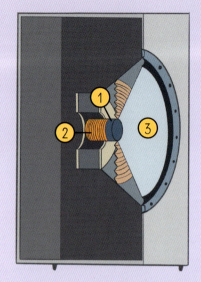

Magnet (1), coil (2), and diaphragm (3) inside a speaker.

Microphone

The microphone a singer sings into actually functions a lot like a speaker. Inside the microphone, there's a thin diaphragm under the round part at the end. Connected to it is a small magnet wrapped in wire. When you speak into the microphone, your voice moves the diaphragm and the magnet. This movement generates in the coil an electrical signal – which is like a tiny invisible wave that carries sound and messages. This weak "signal" is then amplified – meaning it's made louder – so that everyone can hear you clearly.

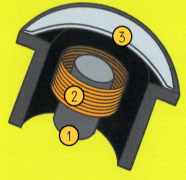

Magnet (1), coil (2), and diaphragm (3) in a microphone.

The human voice

The human voice is like a musical instrument you always have with you. It functions similar to a wind instrument, controlling the airflow as you exhale. Your vocal cords do this by forming a small slit that opens and closes rapidly, allowing us to speak. Surprisingly, the vocal cords don't mind the direction of the airflow, so you can even talk while breathing in. However, it's not very easy – and not ideal for your vocal cords.

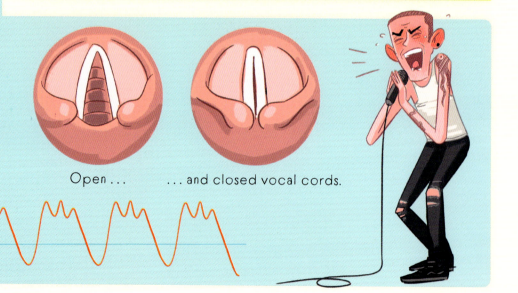

Open... ...and closed vocal cords.

High notes and low notes

A violin plays higher notes than a bass, and you can tell that even without playing them. High notes come from something vibrating quickly, and it's easier for small and light objects to vibrate fast. Low notes, on the other hand, come from things moving more slowly. A bass has longer, thicker strings than a violin and needs a bigger body so that its low notes can resonate.

Who is this . . . ?

Have you ever noticed how a church organ has lots of different pipes? Well, the high notes are made by tiny pipes, the size of your pinkie, while the lowest notes come from pipes several feet long. High notes can sometimes sound unpleasant, but we need them to tell different sounds apart. It's important to know if a car is beeping its horn or an ambulance is wailing. High notes help us recognize different people by their voices, but a telephone is bad at transmitting them, making it hard to tell who's calling.

We all hear low notes well – sometimes too well. If we're disturbed at night by a loud concert, it's the low notes – the pounding drums and the wobbly bass – that keep us awake. Low notes travel well around corners, so there's no escaping them. If they're loud enough, we can feel them vibrating through our whole body. A note can be so low that we no longer hear it, but we still feel it, and these sounds can make people uncomfortable. That's why they are sometimes used in horror films.

7. AT THE POOL

Take the plunge and experience the sights and sounds of the underwater world. Notice how the light ripples with the surface of the water and how the shouts of children and parents seem incredibly far away. Feel how the water cools your whole body down. So take a deep breath and observe.

Sounds beneath the surface

Dive into a pool or your bath and listen carefully. The voices of people from above will fade away, but you'll notice odd, low-pitched sounds. Sound doesn't travel easily from air to water, but it does pass through metal or wood into the water. So, underwater, we easily hear sounds made "in" or "on" the pool or bathtub. But we can barely hear what's happening above the surface.

A life buoy

If you don't know how to swim yet, you can use inflatable rings and armbands to avoid sinking. They're filled with air, which is light and makes you *buoyant*, which means "able to float." Lifejackets on boats and planes work the same way. We even use big inflatable bags to lift sunken submarines and ships from the ocean floor.

From wet to dry

Do you shiver when you get out of the water? Often, people don't want to get out of a swimming pool, but when they do, they quickly reach for a towel to dry off. Once they're dry, they feel warmer. It's because of the water droplets on our skin. Even without a towel, we gradually dry off as the droplets evaporate. But for that to happen, they need warmth, and they take it from our body.

Breaststroke or backstroke

There are loads of interesting things about swimming, but let's start with the basics. How do we actually swim? To move forward in the water, you have to push the water back. Notice how when you swim, you cup your hands into a bowl shape. That's so you can scoop up as much water as possible and move it behind you. And you also kick your legs for the same reason. You're actually pushing yourself further and further away from the water. Looks so simple, doesn't it? Well, it really is, and you'll see this in action just about everywhere. Car wheels push off the road, you push off the ground when you walk, and even rockets dump burning fuel behind them that lifts them high into space. Without this simple principle of "action and reaction," we wouldn't manage to swim or walk very far.

The disappearing experiment

Want to see a cool trick you can do to bend light at home? Get a dish and place a coin inside it, near the rim. Fill a glass with water. While holding the water, position yourself so that the coin has just disappeared from view below the rim of the dish. When you can no longer see the coin, start slowly pouring water into the dish. The light will start to bend in the water and the coin will soon reappear into your view. Amazing, right?

But it's right there . . .

Not where it seems

When you peer into the water, things may not be exactly where they seem. Light behaves differently when it moves from air to water, making objects appear shifted. So, if you're standing at the water's edge and trying to grab a stone from the bottom, you need to reach a bit closer than it appears. The same happens when you look up from underwater: everything seems slightly farther away.

DON'T LOSE YOUR HEAD

Sunshine & invisible light

ALL THE COLORS OF THE RAINBOW
You've surely seen a rainbow before, right? It's like a beautiful painting in the sky, made up of colors from sunlight. But did you know that sunlight has even more colors than what we see in a rainbow? We call these unseen colors "radiation". Beyond the color red in sunlight is what we call "infrared radiation." It's the part of sunlight that warms us up. At the other extreme, beyond the color purple, is what we call "ultraviolet radiation."

THE SUN GIVES US VITAMINS
UV light isn't always a bad thing. Sometimes, it's actually really helpful. It helps our bodies make vitamin D, which is super important for keeping us healthy. It boosts our immunity, which means it helps our bodies fight off sickness. That's why spending time outside, soaking up some sun, is a good idea. Just make sure to be careful if the sun is very strong, so you don't get sunburned.

TOO MUCH SUN IS BAD FOR US
Our atmosphere does a great job protecting us from really strong radiation. But sometimes, the sun is still so strong that we need to be careful. That's why we use sunscreen. It's like a shield that stops the sun's UV light from reaching our skin and giving us sunburns. Some sunglasses also have a special filter that blocks UV light from reaching our eyes. Even regular glass can block some UV light, which is why you don't get much of a tan when you're behind a window. But underwater, UV light can still reach us easily, so we have to be extra careful when we're swimming or snorkeling.

BEWARE OF REFLECTIONS
Watch out when you're in places where sunlight can bounce off surfaces easily, as it can burn your skin. It's also true in winter when there's snow all around. So if you spend all day on a sunny slope in winter, it's smart to use sunscreen to protect your skin.

The energy of light

The colors in a rainbow are actually organized by their energy levels. Red has the least energy, and violet the most. This energy pattern extends beyond what we can see. As we've already mentioned, beyond red, there's the lower-energy radiation we call infrared light. But even lower than that are the waves through which songs travel over long distances to reach your ears – radio waves. On the other hand, ultraviolet (UV) light, which has more energy than violet, can sometimes be harmful. Then there are X-rays and gamma radiation, both with even higher energy levels, which we encounter in places like hospitals and nuclear power stations.

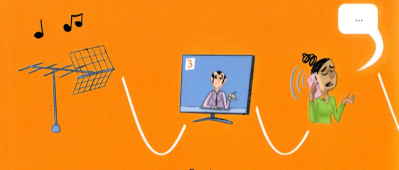

Radio waves

Why does water buoy us up?

BUOYANCY

Water is remarkable. When you dip into it, you feel lighter. The more of your body is underwater, the more it lifts you. This happens with everything submerged, whether it's a fish, a stone, or an inflatable ball. But why does an inflatable ball stay afloat while a stone sinks? It's not just about weight; it's about what things are made of. Light and little things like sand sink because they're denser than water, while big and heavy trees float because they're less dense than water.

Since air is lighter than water, it helps lift everything in it. Our bodies are somewhere in the middle – not as dense as sand, but denser than wood. Your body, being mostly water, naturally floats. But people differ too. Muscular folks don't float as well as those with more fat. Try it yourself: lie on your back in water. Some find it easy, but those with more muscle might struggle and find the water reaches their nose.

The floating experiment

Try putting an orange in water at home. You'll see that it just floats there on the surface of the water. This is because its peel has air trapped inside, which helps it float, similar to how an inflatable ring supports you. However, if you take off the peel and then put the orange in the water again, it will sink. That's because the skin is no longer adding buoyancy. You can also try watching and comparing how other fruits act in water. For example, you can try with a lemon and a lime, a banana and a melon, or an apple and a pear. Which ones do you think will float, and which ones will sink?

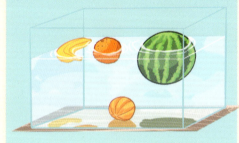

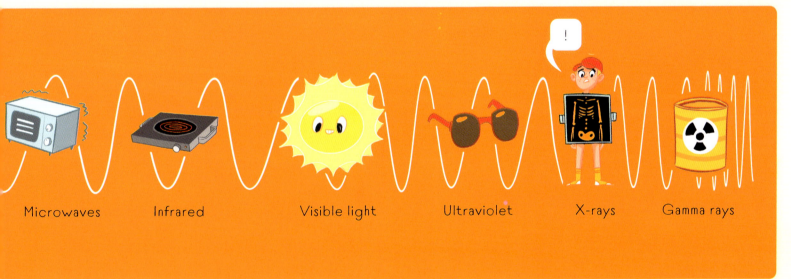

Microwaves · Infrared · Visible light · Ultraviolet · X-rays · Gamma rays

8. AT THE SPORTS FIELD

In sports, we give our all to do our best. We aim to throw farther, jump higher, and run faster. The secret to success is lots of practice and training. But knowing why we do what we do can also make a big difference.

A flying saucer

What's that flying through the air? Is it a UFO? To make your frisbee fly straight and true, you've got to master two moves. As you throw the frisbee forward, you also give it a good spin. When it spins fast, it stays steady in the air. A perfectly thrown frisbee acts like a tiny airplane. As it sails through the air, because of the spinning motion, the air itself helps lift it up.

FLOW

Hitting a ball

A tennis ball needs to be just the right weight. If it's too heavy, it won't move through the air properly. But if it's too light, the wind might blow it away. The top tennis players can serve a ball as fast as a speeding car! It's really tough to hit back a ball coming at you that fast – and the other player has to stop it and hit it back just as fast! It's all about using your elbow, which gets a lot of action during the game.

SPEED

Strong gymnasts on the rings

Have you ever seen a gymnast performing on gymnastic rings? Their routines are so tough that even many super-strong bodybuilders couldn't do them. When a gymnast balances on the rings, they have to lift their whole body weight. Sounds easy, right? But try it yourself. When you hang normally, your arms are pulling together, which is easy. But when you spread your hands as far apart as you can? That's when it gets tough – really tough. Now your arms have to push sideways too. The farther apart your hands are, the harder it gets. That's why it's amazing to watch gymnasts. They make it look so easy.

FORCES

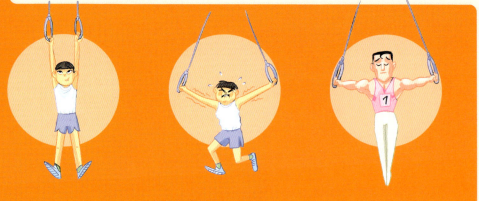

Skating on wheels

When you're new to rollerblading, falling is almost inevitable. As you get more comfortable on your skates, though, try this fun experiment with a friend: stand facing each other and push off against each other gently. If you weigh the same, you'll move away from each other at the same speed. But if one of you is lighter, that person they will move faster. Imagine if an elephant and a mouse were on rollerblades together. The elephant wouldn't budge and the mouse would go sliding back.

The greatest runner

Running comes naturally to us humans. Our skeletons and muscles are perfectly built for it. In fact, over a long enough distance, a trained long-distance runner can even outrun a horse! It's no surprise that in ancient times, Roman runners would deliver important messages over long distances about battles. Even today, some African tribes still use endurance running for hunting. Surprisingly, even if you're not trained, it's not too hard to outrun a dog. Just keep chasing after it. Eventually, the dog will get tired and stop running away.

"You'll sleep well after this, won't you?"

Passing a soccer ball

Scoring a goal in soccer isn't just about kicking the ball where you want it to go. In soccer, teamwork is all about passing. Players must guess ahead of time where the ball and their teammate will meet. In a split-second, a soccer player must kick the ball in the right direction, with the right amount of force. If they had to calculate it on paper, it would take much, much longer. When a soccer player fails to pass accurately, their teammates must adjust their speed.

How to throw as far as possible

It takes practice. When you throw a ball, it moves as fast as your arm. But speed alone isn't enough. How high you throw the ball matters too. The best angle depends on what you're throwing. What's the best angle, then, for throwing a ball? First, try throwing it straight up. Watch your head! Even if the ball stays in the air a long time, it'll land close to where it started. If you throw it forward at arm level, it goes away from you but falls quickly and rolls. You get the longest throw by combining these two angles. Throw the ball both upward and forward at the same time – ideally halfway between these two angles. Athletes don't use protractors to measure their angles, though. It's through practice that they develop a feel for the right way to throw.

One ball is not like another

Producing the right ball for sports like tennis, golf, and soccer is quite a challenge. The rules say how big, heavy, and flexible the ball should be and what it should be made of. Even tiny changes to a ball can affect the outcome of a tournament. Balls take a real beating during games, especially when hit with a bat or racquet, which makes them move much faster than if they were just thrown. Why? The longer the racquet, the more speed you can put on the ball. Try swinging a racquet and notice what moves faster – your

Throwing a frisbee is different than throwing a ball or a javelin. That's because a frisbee behaves differently in the air. If you throw a frisbee too high, it might come back to you like a boomerang. It's hard to find the perfect angle. With practice, though, you'll see the angle is a bit flatter than the angle when you throw a ball. Today's athletes usually focus on distance rather than accuracy.

You'd think athletes would strive to throw things farther and farther. And they do. Except in javelin throwing, that is. The problem in this sport was that the throwers were throwing their javelins too far. German javelin thrower Uwe Hohn even threw a javelin clear across the stadium – so far, it could have landed on the track... or worse, among spectators! For this reason, javelins were changed to limit their distance. The new javelins now have their center of gravity slightly closer to the tip, causing them to tilt down sooner and thus not fly as far. The record books were restarted, and thankfully, now spectators at javelin competitions are safe again.

The impact experiment

A golf ball can travel twice as fast as the end of a golf club. The way it squashes and rebounds happens so quickly that you can't see it with the naked eye. But you can try it out with a tennis ball. Cover one with chalk and then throw it at a wall as hard as you can. You'll see a large mark where the ball hit, showing how much it squashes on impact.

arm or the end of the racquet? After hitting the ball, it moves faster than the racquet because the racquet and the player are much heavier. The ball's flexibility also plays a role. When hit, it gets squashed flat for a moment and then rebounds off the racquet as it returns to its original shape.

It's going to be a personal best.

WHACK!

9. AT THE DOCTOR'S

Sometimes we feel scared about going to the doctor. That's why it's best to ask questions about everything. And if you ask enough questions, you can learn a lot of interesting stuff.

RADIATION

It also works without touch

Imagine a hot burner on a stove. As the ring heats up, it glows red, and you can see from a distance that it's hot. If you switch it off, it goes dark after a moment. But it's still hot, and you can burn yourself on it for a while longer. It's the same with all warm things when they're really hot. But devices called thermometers can see the warm glow from much cooler things, like your body. You point it at someone's forehead, and you know their temperature right away.

Surely he can't be that cold.

SOUND

Breathe deeply

When the doctor checks your body, they often listen to it too. They want to hear how your heart beats, how you're breathing, and how your stomach is working. To hear even the smallest sounds, they use what's called a stethoscope. It's like earbuds but with a wider end they place on your chest. The cold part touching your body has a thin membrane – a diaphragm connected to a tube. When your body makes a sound, it makes the diaphragm vibrate. The diaphragm is big and the tube is small, and that's deliberate. When the sound is channeled into the narrow part, it makes it louder. That way, they can hear what's happening inside you to see if you're healthy.

Take a closer look

Have you ever looked at things up close with a magnifying glass? Try it sometime with a leaf or your fingertip. A magnifying glass shows lots of details. But to see much smaller things – like, say, the tiny cells in the body – we need more than a magnifying glass. That's where microscopes come in. They have two magnifying glasses: an eyepiece and what's called an objective lens. The objective lens makes a bigger image of things, and the eyepiece takes that image and makes it even way bigger. With a microscope, we can magnify things up to a thousand times. That's roughly like a flea blowing up into a hippo!

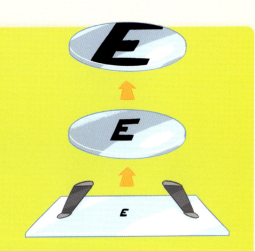

A microscope uses two lenses.

A wing under a magnifying glass...

...under a microscope...

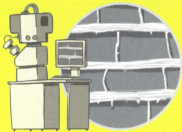

...and in an electron microscope.

When scientists need a really detailed image of something, they don't just shine a light on it. Instead, they use tiny electrons to strike the object. This gives them super detailed pictures so they can study things like viruses and search for cures for diseases.

Have you got a temperature?

Having your temperature taken can be a bit annoying. When you put a glass thermometer under your arm, you have to hold it tightly there for a while. Even with digital thermometers, you might have to wait a few minutes after it beeps to get the results. Measuring temperatures simply takes time. When you measure length, you don't have to wait for the ruler to grow. But for a thermometer to measure your body temperature, it first needs to warm up to match your body heat. And if you don't hold the thermometer properly, you'll end up measuring the room's temperature instead.

Take a peek inside

If a doctor wants to see what's hidden inside you, there are a few ways they can do this. For example, they can send out a sound and see how it bounces off you. Or they can use radiation and watch where it goes through you and comes out the other side. These are called ultrasound and X-rays!

The echo of our bodies

To listen to our bodies, doctors use a really high-pitched sound called ultrasound. It's so high that not even the most sensitive human ears can hear it. In general, human hearing isn't all that great. Dogs, dolphins, and bats, for instance, can hear higher pitches than we can. This means that we can summon a dog using an ultrasonic whistle that doesn't disturb people but will bring that pooch bounding up at once. Furthermore, dolphins and bats get their bearings straight with an ability we call echolocation – using echoes to find out where things are. The bat simply makes a sound, which bounces off the things all around it and comes back again to the bat. Depending on how long it takes the sound to return, the bat learns how far away trees, caves, and even food are. In a sense, it can "see" using its ears – how cool is that?!

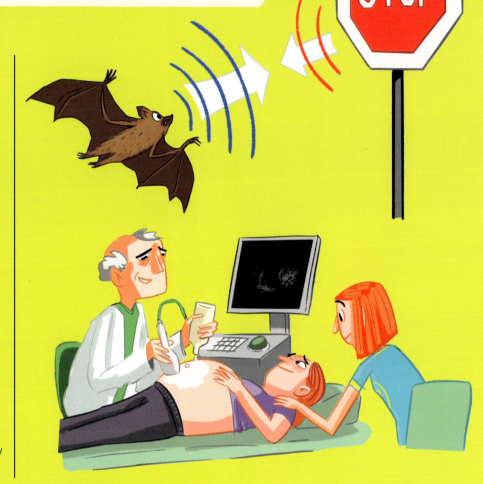

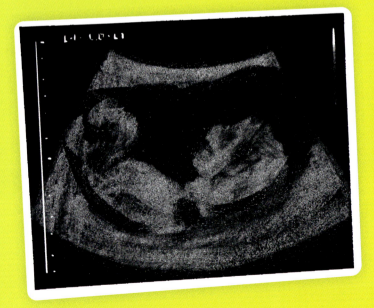

To make such a high-pitched sound, something small and light has to vibrate faster than any of the musical instruments we are familiar with. During an ultrasound scan, gel is applied to make sure the sound waves can penetrate the body well. This lets us listen to echoes from inside the body. And because we're listening to the sound reflected, we can see the boundaries between different materials – actually, just the outlines of bone and tissue. Ultrasound is commonly used to examine the stomach, heart, and even babies who haven't been born yet. Ask your parents – they might have your sweet little ultrasound baby picture stashed away somewhere.

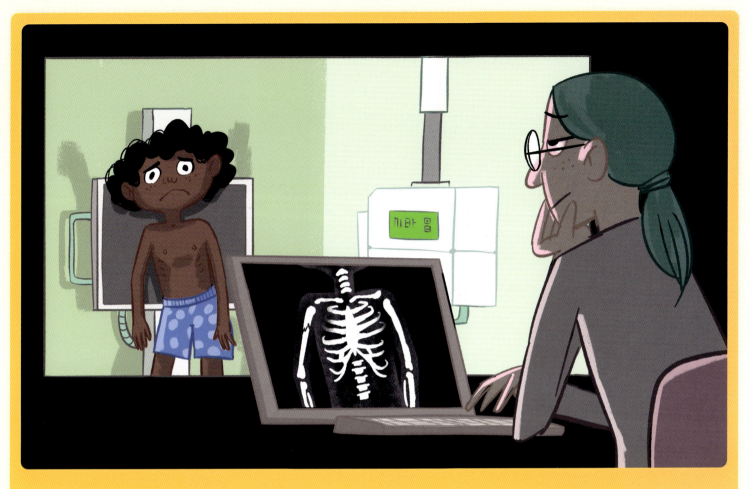

The mysterious X-rays

Doctors use many clever ways to see inside our bodies. For example, they sometimes shine a kind of light on your body to take a picture. But instead of using a flashlight, they use a special kind of radiation called X-rays. X-rays can pass through the air and the soft parts of your body (your muscles, your organs, and your skin) but not your bones, so they create an image showing your bones in white, your soft tissue in gray, and the air in black. This helps doctors find broken bones or conditions like pneumonia. For more detailed views, doctors use CT scans – taking X-rays from different angles to create a 3D image. While X-rays have more energy than sunlight and can be harmful, the amount used during an examination is small and safe. Doctors also protect your sensitive areas with lead plates. Those doctors who work with X-rays every day have to be much more careful. That's why they go into another room when they're taking a photo of you.

10. IN A SHOP

Shopping can feel like a dull chore sometimes, right? But have you ever wondered how to ride a shopping cart like a pro? Or what's up with that mysterious light on the conveyor belt at the checkout counter? And have you ever noticed how vibrant and detailed dollar bills can be?

Beeeep!

A barcode in a shop can be read by a thing called a scanner. It shines a red light that reflects off the white parts but not the black ones. It's actually these white stripes that the machine sees. To make sure the scanner knows it's reading a code and not, say, a stripey shirt, the stripes at either end have a specific thickness. In a square QR code, the top left corner is also marked to show where the code begins.

Black and white stripes

You've probably noticed that things sold in shops have these little squares on them, a bit bigger than a postage stamp. It's a unique code for each item, a bit like a fingerprint. It contains digital information about the price and the type of item so that the sellers can keep track of their goods. Sometimes they also use other square codes, called QR codes. These contain the code for a website, which you can then read on a smartphone.

A ticket with a barcode.

A ticket with a QR code.

Security lock

In stores, clothes and electronics often have a plastic tag that sets off an alarm if you try to leave without paying. It's a simple way to stop people from stealing. But sometimes, the tag isn't removed at the store after something is purchased. If that happens, you can try using a strong magnet to unlock it. Shop assistants use magnets to remove the tags too.

BEEEP!

Yep, on special offer.

The conveyor belt

Have you ever wondered how checkout conveyor belts know when to stop moving? At one end, there are two strange parts facing each other over the belt. One emits invisible infrared light, and the other has a sensor that sees if the light is shining on it. If the sensor sees the light, the belt keeps moving. But if something, like a cucumber, blocks the light, the sensor notices and stops the belt. It's like how automatic doors open or water flows from a tap at a public restroom without you touching anything.

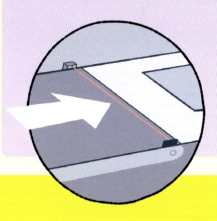

A heavy load

You can have a lot of fun with a shopping cart. When you've got lots of shopping to do, it's smart to think about where to put the heavy stuff so you can steer easily. If you put them near the handle, you'll need more strength to turn the cart, but you'll have better control. If you put heavy things farther away, you'll have to turn it differently. Just keep the front wheels steady and use the back to turn the cart. Then push. It'll be harder to control overall, though. That's why they put the baby seat near the handle.

41

Are we weighing things accurately?

How can we be sure that the pound of apples we bought in a store really weighs a pound? Are the scales in the shop even accurate? How do we make sure everyone weighs things the same way? And is a pound the same all over the world?

You might go to a shop to buy a pound of cheese, a gallon of milk, or a few feet of two-by-four-inch wood. You know there are 12 ounces in one pound as there are 12 inches in one foot. But how big exactly is a foot and how heavy is a pound? In medieval times, it was common for each city to have its own units of measurement. This led to much confusion – the same rope could be 15 feet long in one city and 18 feet long somewhere else. In medieval England, a pound was originally defined as the weight of 7,000 grains of barley. And based on the law of an English king, one inch was meant to be as long as three

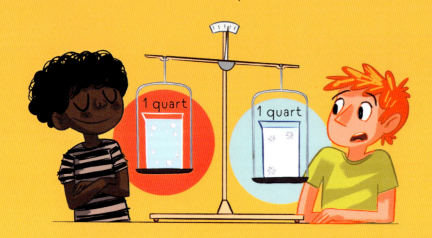

How do we protect banknotes?

Take a good look at a dollar bill sometime. It's fascinating how many different features they have on them. There are even some you can't see. You may have wondered why that is. If banknotes were made in an ordinary way, anyone could print them. Forging banknotes has to be difficult, so each country has come up with lots of clever features to protect its banknotes.

Banknotes aren't made from regular paper – they're way, way tougher! Hold one up to the light and you might spot a watermark – a hidden picture you can't see on the surface.

watermark

grains of barley placed lengthwise. As trade bloomed, it was necessary to agree to some standard. So governments started to create etalons – a prime example of one pound, one foot, or another unit. Each state could use that standard to make a precise copy and be able to measure the same results as anyone else. So you can have a lot of weights exactly one pound heavy. All of them would be "a pound" but there once was "the pound".

In the United States, we are used to pounds, inches, feet, miles, and degrees Fahrenheit. Most of the world uses different units, though – meters, kilograms, or degrees Celsius. There is nothing wrong with using different units for measurement. In fact, we have three different miles: the mile, the US survey mile, and the nautical mile, all different. We just have to maintain our standards so we can convert easily between any two units. It basically boils down to familiarity and convenience. In the end, it was more convenient to leave behind our own standards of the pound and the foot. They still exist, but nowadays we define one pound as an exact portion of one kilogram and one foot as an exact portion of one meter.

IR

To safeguard banknotes, special measures are taken using infrared light, which, as we've discussed, is a kind of light we can't see. Different strips or designs are added, like the ones on dollar bills. Unlike banknotes in Europe, US dollars are all the same size. But machines can tell them apart easily using infrared light.

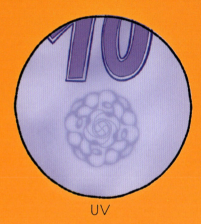

UV

Most banknotes have hidden printing on them that becomes visible under ultraviolet (UV) light, which, like infrared light, is also invisible. Shop assistants use a UV device to check banknotes for authenticity. Under this purple light, some shapes glow, and hidden designs on the banknote become visible. It's quite fascinating to see!

thread

Banknotes can have colored fibers or a metallic thread in them. Look closely – there might be tiny writing you can only see with a magnifying glass, and some pictures might change color when you tilt the note.

GLOSSARY

Buoyancy

When things are put into water, they might sink, float, or stay on the surface. Whatever the result, water always buoys things up. It's just that sometimes that's enough and sometimes it isn't. What's important here is the material we throw into the water. But water isn't the only thing that can make things float; the air around us also supports our weight on land. It is subtle, but it becomes clear with large, light objects like hot-air balloons.

Changes of state

We're familiar with water in the form of drops, but also as ice or steam. That's because it exists in three states: liquid (water), solid (ice), and gas (steam). When ice is heated, it melts into water. Further heating then turns water into steam. This ability to transition between states applies to all substances, each requiring specific temperatures and amounts of heat to transform.

Electricity

It's impossible to imagine the modern world without electricity. That's why we bring it into our homes using cables, although in cities this isn't immediately obvious. But if you want to see the cables, all you have to do is look up and follow the route of a utility pole or a streetlight. Electricity often works for us, but it can also provide us with plenty of entertainment – from powering the rides at an amusement park to a concert by your favorite band.

Energy transformations

Sometimes people feel like they've got no energy. But energy can't just vanish. It's only converted into a different form. You can use the energy of your muscles to kick a ball, thus making it move fast. You can warm your hands with friction by rubbing them together. At other times, energy remains stored after we've put in the effort and we can use it later. For instance, when we go down a hill or when we release a coiled spring.

Equilibrium

Nature seeks equilibrium. This refers to a state it can easily remain in for a long time without any changes. For instance, balancing a ball on your nose is difficult. Whenever it tips over, it falls on the ground. And nature is satisfied. It cannot fall any lower. If we want a result other than equilibrium, we have to make an effort and keep up that effort. On a playground swing, your muscles will take you far, then nature brings you back to the lowest point.

Flow

This is a concept you'll find in both air and water, or anything else that flows. In physics, these substances are called fluids. When air moves, it can be either a gentle breeze or a strong wind – both in nature and when we create it ourselves, like when playing a flute or trumpet. When air flows, it can also set things in motion, like leaves blown by the wind or even airplanes and frisbees, all of which rely on air flow to work.

Forces

When we apply force, we can move or even squash something. But watch out – everything you use force on will also apply force against you. For instance, if you fall hitting the ground, the ground hits you. Forces are fair like that: they always act in both directions with the same amount of strength. Forces help us twist things too, and where you push or pull is also important.

Light

We can think of light as a bunch of rays shooting out in every direction from sources like the sun, a fire, or a lamp. These rays fly straight until something gets in their way. A mirror will reflect the rays in the direction we want. Water that stands in the way of the rays will bend them and deflect them from their direction. In this way, light can reach places it wouldn't otherwise reach.

Measuring

When we really want to know things precisely, we have to measure them. The better we want to know something, the more precise tools we need. But it's not just about having these tools. We need to agree on how to use them worldwide so that we can all understand each other and make sure we're measuring things the same way – whether we're in a science lab or in a store. We have to be careful when we measure, though. We have to make sure we're really measuring what we want and not making mistakes.

Pressure

Do you ever feel under a lot of pressure? Well, you are – literally. The air above you is pressing down on you. Even though the air is light, there's a whole lot of it. We don't notice its pressure because we're used to it. Imagine layers of bricks in a wall instead of air. It's clear that the lower layers have to withstand a lot of pressure from the bricks above. If we want to reduce pressure, we need smaller forces to act on as large an area as possible.

Radiation

As we move beyond the visible colors of the rainbow, our eyes can't detect anything. But even the parts we can't see impact us. All light, whether we see it or not, is called radiation. Some kinds, like infrared, can make you feel warm and cozy. But watch out for ultraviolet radiation – it can give you a nasty sunburn! We use invisible radiation in all sorts of things, like automatic doors at shops and even water taps. It's a clever way to make things work without bothering us with bright lights.

Sound

Sound helps us chat with friends and enjoy calming tunes. It even lets us see images of unborn babies through ultrasound. But loud sounds can be annoying or even harmful. Sound usually travels through the air, but it can also reach us underwater or through solid objects, sounding a bit different but still getting the message across.

Speed

Speed is exciting too. Whether it's zooming on a bike, cruising in a car, or enjoying a thrilling amusement park attraction, people love speed. But in reality, we're more aware of accelerating, braking, or turning sharply than we are of speed itself. Quick acceleration pushes us into our seats, and racing downhill gives us that stomach-flipping feeling. When we're cruising at a steady speed, like on the highway, it feels smooth and easy. But when we have to brake suddenly, that's when our speed can catch us off guard.

Work

When it comes to getting things done, we have plenty of options: we can use our brains, muscles, or machines. Physicists, though, are specifically interested in tasks that involve moving things around, like heavy materials on a construction site. Some might say that as long as we get the job done, the method doesn't matter. But our muscles strongly – so to speak – disagree. They care deeply about how we accomplish a task. Sometimes, brute strength is necessary. When that's not enough, though, we can turn to tools like planks or pulleys to make the job easier. This might take more time, but it's all about finding the best path that works for us.

THE AMAZING THEATRE OF PHYSICS is an entertainment and educational group that performs science experiments in order to show people how the world around us works in a way that is fun and exciting. They're like magicians, only they explain how their tricks work. Having started performing in 2008, they travel around the world with their show, performing in a wide range of venues, from theaters, town squares, and schools to churches, synagogues, and retirement homes. This work is based on their lifelong research and experience.

A quick word on the inspiration for this book:

The world in which we live is governed by the laws of nature, and people's lives have improved whenever they've begun to understand something more about them. This is why it is important to observe the world around you and take note of interesting phenomena and the connections between them. And that's why we wrote this book. It attempts to show physics phenomena in the places where we might encounter them and explain their causes and effects. Many things and phenomena have their own names in physics. It is good to know them, but naming things in itself doesn't mean understanding them. That's why this book avoids technical terms and tries to describe the laws of nature as simply as possible – though not simplistically. We believe that the world is more beautiful when you know how it works.

Links with commentary:

Have you tried all the experiments in the book? Did you enjoy them and want to try out more? Check out these websites.

- Make physics toys from material you'd normally find at home. All you need are a few bits and pieces and a little time, and you'll find so much to explore.
  www.arvindguptatoys.com

- Instructables has instructions for lots of different projects – from simple to sophisticated, creative to technical. They've been made by enthusiastic people getting together, and you can join in too.
  www.instructables.com

- Head to the science centre and explore their exhibits and programmes. Or at least have a look at their website as you'll often find interesting tips for experiments and activities. We recommend this website from the Exploratorium in San Francisco.
  www.exploratorium.edu/explore/activities

Do you want to watch experiments as well as read about them? Check out these videos.

- Homemade Science offers lots of things to explore, try out and make.
  www.youtube.com/@YeanyScience/videos

- Are you interested in the latest scientific trends and the most up-to-date findings? Then don't miss the annual Christmas Lecture from the Royal Institution in London, where they try to make science more accessible to all viewers, regardless of age or education.
  www.rigb.org/christmas-lectures

- Is it true? Can it really work like that? Or is it just a myth or legend? Explore together with MythBusters.
  www.imdb.com/title/tt0383126

- Veritasium brings you interesting facts from the world of physics, technology and mathematics. Concepts which at first sight may seem illogical are explained and discussed with scientists, and in the process of exploring them, the camera takes you to places you normally wouldn't have access to.
  www.youtube.com/@veritasium

- Minute Physics uses short animated videos to explain complex phenomena in physics, as well as provide answers to tricky questions.
  www.youtube.com/user/minutephysics

I want to go back.

THE AWESOME PHYSICS IN YOUR CITY

© B4U Publishing for Albatros,
an imprint of Albatros Media Group, 2025
5. května 1746/22, Prague 4, Czech Republic
Written by The Amazing Theatre of Physics
Illustrations © Tomáš Kopecký
Translated by Graeme Dibble
Edited by Scott Alexander Jones

Printed in China by Leo Paper Group Ltd.

www.albatrosbooks.com

All rights reserved.
Reproduction of any content is strictly prohibited without the written permission of the rights holders.